STAR MATHS TOOLS

Interactive maths made easy

TERMS AND CONDITIONS

IMPORTANT – PERMITTED USE AND WARNINGS – READ CAREFULLY BEFORE USING

Copyright in the software contained in the CD-ROM and in its accompanying material belongs to Scholastic Limited. All rights reserved. © 2009 Scholastic Ltd.

Save for these purposes, or as expressly authorised in the accompanying materials, the software may not be copied, reproduced, used, sold, licensed, transferred, exchanged, hired, or exported in whole or in part or in any manner or form without the prior written consent of Scholastic Ltd. Any such unauthorised use or activities are prohibited and may give rise to civil liabilities and criminal prosecutions.

The material contained on the CD-ROM may only be used in the context for which it was intended in *Star Maths Tools*, and is for use only in the school which has purchased the book and CD-ROM, or by the teacher who has purchased the book and CD-ROM. Permission to download images is given for purchasers only and not for users from any lending service. Any further use of the material contravenes Scholastic Ltd's copyright and that of other rights holders.

The CD-ROM has been tested for viruses at all stages of its production. However, we recommend that you run virus-checking software on your computer systems at all times. Scholastic Ltd cannot accept any responsibility for any loss, disruption or damage to your data or your computer system that may occur as a result of using either the CD-ROM or the data held on it.

IF YOU ACCEPT THE ABOVE CONDITIONS YOU MAY PROCEED TO USE THE CD-ROM.

Minimum specification:
- PC or Mac with a CD-ROM drive and at least 512 Mb RAM (recommended)
- Recommended screen resolution: 1280 × 1024 pixels (see CD-ROM help notes for details)
- Facilities for printing

PC:
- Windows 98SE or above
- Recommended minimum processor speed: 1 GHz

Mac:
- Mac OSX.4 or above
- Recommended minimum processor speed: 1 GHz

For all technical support queries, please phone Scholastic Customer Services on 0845 6039091.

Julie Cogill and Anthony David

Authors
Julie Cogill and Anthony David

Digital Resource Design & Development
Vivid Interactive

Development Editor
Gina Thorsby

Editors
Mary Nathan, Catherine Taylor and Christine Vaughan

Assistant Editor
Margaret Eaton

Series Designers
Joy Monkhouse and Melissa Leeke

Designer
Quadrum Solutions Pvt. Ltd.

Text © 2009 Julie Cogill and Anthony David
© 2009 Scholastic Ltd

Tools © Vivid Interactive Ltd 2009

Designed using Adobe CS

Published by Scholastic Ltd
Villiers House, Clarendon Avenue,
Leamington Spa, Warwickshire CV32 5PR
www.scholastic.co.uk

Printed by Tien Wah, Singapore
1 2 3 4 5 6 7 8 9   9 0 1 2 3 4 5 6 7 8

ISBN 978-1407-10201-6

ACKNOWLEDGEMENTS
Extracts from the Primary National Strategy's *Primary Framework for Mathematics* (2006) www.standards.dfes.gov.uk/primaryframework © Crown copyright. Reproduced under the terms of the Click Use Licence.

The approved SMART Software Accreditation logo is a trademark of SMART Technologies.

Every effort has been made to trace copyright holders for the works reproduced in this book, and the publishers apologise for any inadvertent omissions.

British Library Cataloguing-in-Publication Data
A catalogue record for this book is available from the British Library.

The rights of the authors of this work have been asserted by them in accordance with the Copyright, Designs and Patents Act 1988.

All rights reserved. This book is sold subject to the condition that it shall not, by way of trade or otherwise, be lent, hired out or otherwise circulated without the publisher's prior consent in any form of binding or cover other than that in which it is published and without a similar condition, including this condition, being imposed upon the subsequent purchaser.

No part of this publication may be reproduced, stored in a retrieval system, or transmitted, in any form or by any means, electronic, mechanical, photocopying, recording or otherwise, other than for the purposes described in the lessons in this book, without the prior permission of the publisher. This book remains copyright, although permission is granted to copy pages where indicated for classroom distribution and use only in the school which has purchased the book, or by the teacher who has purchased the book, and in accordance with the CLA licensing agreement. Photocopying permission is given only for purchasers and not for borrowers of books from any lending service.

Introduction 4

Objectives grid 7

Activities

Clocks 9
Activity notes 10
What's the time? 12

Coordinates, reflections and rotations 13
Activity notes 14
Make mine the same! 16

Fraction equivalents 17
Activity notes 18
Fill the gaps 20

Graphs and charts 21
Activity notes 22
Data table 24

Magic calculator 25
Activity notes 26
Missing numbers 28

Number line 29
Activity notes 30
Totals to 10 32

Number square 33
Activity notes 34
Addition square 36

Number words 37
Activity notes 38
Name that number 40

Partition numbers 41
Activity notes 42
Digits and decimals 44

Shape paper 45
Activity notes 46
Find the cubes 48

Introduction

In the CPD programme, *Guide for your professional development: Using ICT to support mathematics in primary schools,* the DfES identified the following as important for teachers in determining whether to use ICT in primary mathematics:

- ICT should enhance good mathematics teaching. It should be used in lessons only if it supports good practice in teaching mathematics.
- Any decision about using ICT in a particular lesson (or sequence of lessons) must be directly related to the teaching and learning objectives for those lessons.
- ICT should be used if the teacher and/or the children can achieve something more effectively with it than without it.

Careful consideration and planning are therefore needed to fulfil the potential of the full range of ICT. HMI have since reported that, although ICT is increasingly available in schools, its effectiveness and appropriate use is variable with too many programs failing to support the teaching and learning of a specific learning objective and often used just for the sake of it!

Using ICT as a demonstration and modelling tool with the whole class is, however, a particularly effective use of technology. The *Star Maths Tools* series is designed to provide classes and teachers with a stimulating bank of interactive resources that can be used to demonstrate and model maths teaching, as well as to explore specific mathematical ideas, concepts and objectives.

About Star Maths Tools

Star Maths Tools is a new series of books with accompanying CD-ROMs that offers teachers a set of highly configurable maths tools for use across the primary maths curriculum. The ten tools on each CD-ROM are accessible to all teachers (however confident they might be in using whiteboard tools) and are designed to:

- provide potential for all children to be actively involved in teaching and learning
- provide potential for teachers to structure and manage interactive maths teaching for a variety of purposes across the maths curriculum.

Each tool in each year group is fully configurable to cover all ability levels. The accompanying teachers' notes also reflect differentiation and progression across a range of PNS renewed Framework objectives. The *Star Maths Tools* will enable teachers to develop a rich bank of teaching activities that fit into their existing planning framework and that can be used to support a range of learning objectives within each year group.

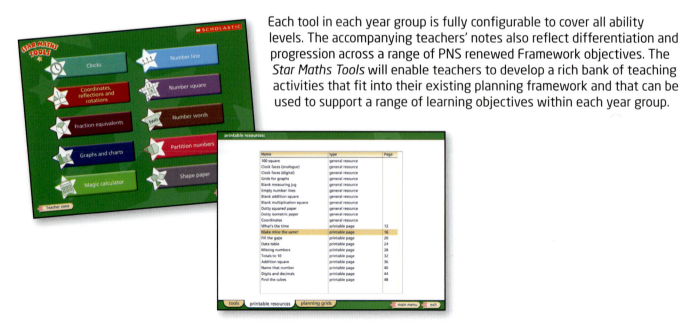

Introduction

About the book

Each book includes a bank of teachers' notes linked to each of the *Star Maths Tools* on the CD-ROM. A photocopiable resource sheet is also provided for each tool to help to reinforce concepts which have been demonstrated or modelled using the tools.

Objectives grid

The planning grid on pages 7–8 provides a comprehensive guide identifying the links in each of the activities to the *Primary Framework for Mathematics* strands and objectives. Text highlighted in blue indicates the end-of-year objectives for the different strands.

Activity pages

A four-page teaching unit is provided for each of the ten tools in the following format:

About the tool

The first page of each unit includes annotated screen shots containing at-a-glance instructions for using the tool. Notes on key tool functions and a brief overview of the possible uses of each tool are also provided.

Activity notes

The second and third pages of each teaching unit include four specific teaching activities. Each activity includes the following notes:

Activity type

The teaching covers a range of different purposes including 'Starter', 'Whole class', 'Review', 'Paired', 'Group' and 'Assessment' activities.

Learning objective

Covering the strands and objectives of the renewed *Primary Framework for Mathematics*. End-of-year objectives are highlighted in blue.

What to do

Outline notes on how to administer the activity with the whole class, groups, pairs and so on.

Key questions

Probing questions to be used during the activity.

Assessment for learning

Key assessment points and criteria for assessing each activity.

Activity resource sheet

The fourth page of each teaching unit is a photocopiable resource sheet (also available in printable format on the CD-ROM). These resource sheets are designed to provide outlines of the tools for recording purposes or to consolidate or extend learning.

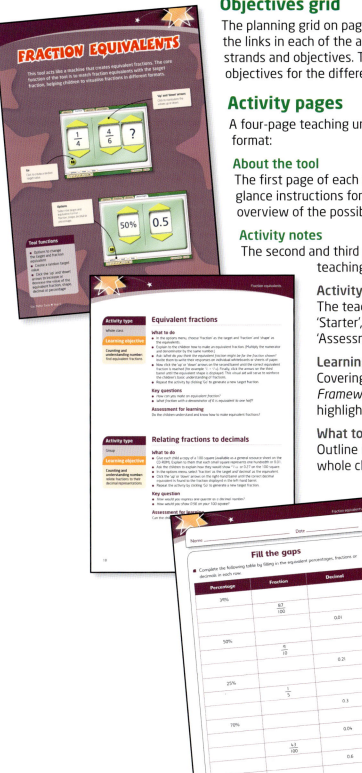

Star Maths Tools ★ Year 5

5

Introduction

About the CD-ROM

The CD-ROM includes the following ten tools:

Clocks

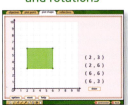
Coordinates, reflections and rotations

Fraction equivalents

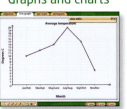
Graphs and charts

Magic calculator

Number line

Number square

Number words

Partition numbers

Shape paper

Objectives screen

The opening screen of each of the ten tools offers teachers the opportunity to type in their own lesson objective.

Teacher's toolbox

All of the activities on the CD-ROM feature a set of interactive whiteboard tools, which include a pen tool, a highlighter tool, a line tool and a notepad for the teacher or child at the board to write questions, answers and a record of workings-out.

Teacher zone

The teachers' section includes links from the tools activities to the *Primary Framework for Mathematics* strands, together with an editable objectives grid provided in Word format, a diary page and printable versions of the worksheets. A selection of general resource sheets for recording work away from the whiteboard or PC is also included.

How to use the CD-ROM

System requirements

Minimum specification
- PC with a CD-ROM drive and 512 Mb RAM (recommended)
- Windows 98SE or above/Mac OSX.4 or above
- Recommended minimum processor speed: 1 GHz

Getting started

The *Star Maths Tools* CD-ROM should auto run when inserted into your CD drive. If it does not, browse to your CD drive to view the contents of the CD-ROM and click on the *Star Maths Tools* icon.

From the start-up screen you will find four options: select **Credits** to view a list of acknowledgements. Click on **Register** to register the product in order to receive product updates and special offers. Click on **How to use** to access support notes for using the CD-ROM. Finally, if you agree to the terms and conditions, select **Start** to move to the main menu.

For all technical support queries, please contact Scholastic Customer Services help desk on 0845 6039091.

Objectives grid

Tool	Page No.	Activity title	Learning objective
Clocks	10	Converting 12- to 24-hour times	**Measuring:** read time using 24-hour clock notation
	10	To the nearest minute	**Measuring:** read time to the nearest minute using an analogue display; read time using 24-hour clock notation
	11	Using a calendar	**Measuring:** use a calendar to calculate time intervals
	11	How much older?	**Measuring:** use a calendar to calculate time intervals
Coordinates, reflections and rotations	14	Coordinates	**Understanding shape:** read and plot coordinates in the first quadrant
	14	Parallel and perpendicular lines	**Understanding shape:** recognise parallel and perpendicular lines in grids and shapes
	15	Four-sided shapes	**Understanding shape:** identify, visualise and describe properties of rectangles and regular polygons
	15	Reflections	**Understanding shape:** draw the position of a shape after a reflection
Fraction equivalents	18	Equivalent fractions	**Counting and understanding number:** find equivalent fractions
	18	Relating fractions to decimals	**Counting and understanding number:** relate fractions to their decimal representations
	19	Percentages to decimals	**Counting and understanding number:** relate fractions to their decimal representations; express tenths and hundredths as percentages
	19	Percentages as fractions	**Counting and understanding number:** express tenths and hundredths as percentages
Graphs and charts	22	Understanding line graphs	**Handling data:** construct line graphs to represent changes over time; identify further questions to ask
	22	Creating bar charts	**Handling data:** answer a set of related questions by collecting, selecting and organising relevant data; draw conclusions, using ICT to present features
	23	Finding the mode	**Handling data:** find and interpret the mode of a set of data
	23	Interpreting pictograms	**Handling data:** draw conclusions, using ICT to present features, and identify further questions to ask
Magic calculator	26	Finding fractions	**Calculating:** use a calculator to solve problems, including those involving fractions; interpret the display correctly in the context of measurement
	26	Multiplying by 10, 100 or 1000	**Calculating:** use understanding of place value to multiply whole numbers by 10, 100 or 1000
	27	Dividing by 10 or 100	**Calculating:** use understanding of place value to divide whole numbers by 10 or 100
	27	Finding percentages	**Calculating:** find percentages of numbers

Objectives grid

Tool	Page No.	Activity title	Learning objective
Number line	30	Counting beyond zero	**Counting and understanding number:** count from any given number in whole-number and decimal steps, extending beyond zero when counting backwards
		Decimal pairs that add to 10	**Knowing and using number facts:** use knowledge of place value and addition and subtraction of two-digit numbers to derive sums and differences of decimals
	31	Rounding to the nearest number	**Counting and understanding number:** explain what each digit represents in a number with up to two decimal places, and round these numbers
		Reading partially labelled scales	**Measuring:** interpret a reading that lies between two unnumbered divisions on a scale
Number square	34	Pairs of factors	**Knowing and using number facts:** identify pairs of factors of two-digit whole numbers
		Times tables	**Knowing and using number facts:** recall quickly multiplication facts up to 10 × 10
	35	Number investigation	**Using and applying mathematics:** explore patterns, properties and relationships and propose a general statement involving numbers
		Mystery squares	**Using and applying mathematics:** explore patterns, properties and relationships and propose a general statement involving numbers
Number words	38	Whole numbers up to 100,000	**Counting and understanding number:** explain what each digit represents in whole numbers
		Reading decimals	**Counting and understanding number:** explain what each digit represents in decimals with up to two places
	39	Find the missing numbers	**Using and applying mathematics:** explore patterns, properties and relationships involving numbers
		Exploring number patterns	**Using and applying mathematics:** explore patterns, properties and relationships involving numbers
Partition numbers	42	Explaining two decimal places	**Counting and understanding number:** explain what each digit represents in whole numbers and decimals with up to two places
		Multiplication	**Calculating:** refine and use efficient written methods to multiply HTU × U
	43	Adding decimal numbers	**Calculating:** use efficient written methods to add whole numbers and decimals with up to two places
		Larger or smaller	**Counting and understanding number:** explain what each digit represents in whole numbers and decimals with up to two places, and order these numbers
Shape paper	46	Nets of a cube	**Understanding shape:** identify and draw nets of 3D shapes
		Tessellating patterns	**Using and applying mathematics:** explore patterns, properties and relationships involving shapes
	47	Lines of symmetry	**Understanding shape:** complete patterns with up to two lines of symmetry
		Finding the area of rectangles	**Measuring:** use the formula for the area of a rectangle to calculate the rectangle's area

CLOCKS

This is a flexible tool that gives users the choice to display either one or two analogue or digital clocks or calendars per screen. The options menu allows the times on any clock to be randomised to the nearest minute, five minutes, 15 minutes, half-hour or hour.

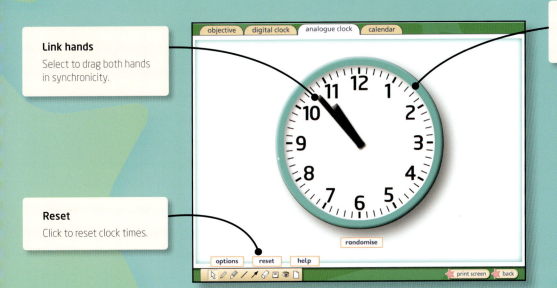

Link hands
Select to drag both hands in synchronicity.

Show numbers/minutes
Show or hide numbers or minute markers.

Reset
Click to reset clock times.

Time set
Adjust hours and minutes separately.

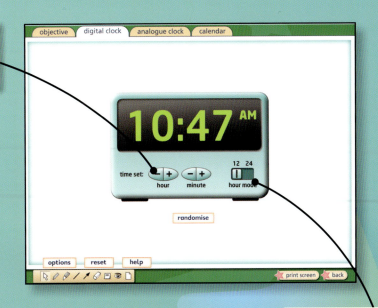

Tool functions

- 'Randomise' creates a random time on each clock
- Numbers or minute markers may be hidden
- Analogue clock hands may be moved to any time
- Digital time may be displayed in 12-hour or 24-hour clock mode
- Dates can be highlighted in different colours

Hour mode
Display 12- or 24-hour times.

Star Maths Tools ★ Year 5

9

Clocks

Activity type

Whole class

Learning objective

Measuring: read time using 24-hour clock notation

Converting 12- to 24-hour times

What to do

- Select the digital clock. Display one digital clock, and select 12-hour clock mode.
- Click 'randomise' to show different times. Ask: *Do you know the meaning of am and pm?* Explain how the 24-hour clock system works: for times after 12 midday, add 12 to the hours (for example, 8:45pm becomes 20:45); for times after midnight, write a zero in front if there is only one 'hours' digit (for example, 7:23am becomes 07:23, and other times stay the same (for example, 11:45am is 11:45).
- Switch between the 12-hour and 24-hour clock using 'hour mode' for different times. Show a time in 12-hour clock mode, and ask the children to write the equivalent 24-hour clock time on their individual whiteboards (or sheets of paper).
- Show different times on the 24-hour clock. Ask the children to write the times in 12-hour clock notation.
- Ask the children to work with partners to complete photocopiable page 12.

Key questions

- *When you see a time in 24-hour clock notation, how can you tell whether it is morning or afternoon?*
- *Why do you think timetables are always written using 24-hour clock notation?*

Assessment for learning

Do the children understand 24-hour clock notation and are they confident in converting between times on the 12-hour and 24-hour clock?

Activity type

Starter

Learning objective

Measuring: read time to the nearest minute using an analogue display; read time using 24-hour clock notation

To the nearest minute

What to do

- Select the analogue clock. In the options menu, choose 'show numbers' and 'show minutes' but not 'link hands', and randomise to the nearest minute.
- Click 'randomise' to show different times. Ask the children to tell the times as accurately as they can to the nearest minute.
- If necessary, drag either the hour hand or the minute hand to help to explain the times shown. For example, for 23 minutes to 4, drag the hour hand to show that the next hour it will reach is 4. (The hands are not linked so the minute hand will stay in its original position.)
- Now return to the options menu and de-select 'show minutes'. Click 'randomise' and ask the children to write each time on their individual whiteboards.
- Extend the session by asking the children to estimate times to the nearest five minutes and to show the times using 12- and 24-hour clock notation.

Key questions

- *Can you tell me the time to the nearest minute?*
- *If I move the hour hand on by three hours, what time will it be?*

Assessment for learning

Can the children tell the time to the nearest minute and estimate time to the nearest five minutes?

Clocks

Using a calendar

Activity type
Whole class

Learning objective
Measuring: use a calendar to calculate time intervals

What to do
- Display the calendar screen. Use the options menu to display two calendars. On the first calendar, highlight two dates in the same month using the whiteboard tools.
- Ask the children to tell you the number of days between the dates. Explain that they can count on, but that subtracting one date from the other is more efficient.
- After several examples using one calendar, click 'reset' and change the month on the calendar on the right-hand side so that it shows one month ahead.
- Highlight a date on the first calendar and another date on the second one.
- Explain that the easiest way to calculate the number of days between two different months is to count the number of days to the end of the first month, and then to add the number of days up to the date in the second month. Repeat with several examples.

Key questions
- *On which date do you start when counting on?*
- *If the first Monday in a month is the 1st, what are the dates of the remaining Mondays in the month?*

Assessment for learning
Are the children clear about methods of counting on and can they calculate time intervals between dates?

How much older?

Activity type
Group

Learning objective
Measuring: use a calendar to calculate time intervals

What to do
- Ask each child in the group for their birthdays and invite them to write these on their individual whiteboards or sheets of paper. Discuss who is the oldest/youngest child, and the age order of all the children in the group.
- Open the calendar screen and display two calendars. On the first calendar, highlight the birthday of the oldest child in the group, and on the other, highlight the birthday of the next oldest child.
- Ask the children to work out by counting on or back (or using other methods) how many months and/or days older one child is than the other.
- Repeat the activity, using the birthdays of two other children in the group.

Key questions
- *If there is a month between two birthdays (for example, the first birthday is in January and the second is in March), how would you calculate the number of days between them?*
- *Why is the difference not the same between birthdays on 14 February and 3 March and between 14 May and 3 June?*

Assessment for learning
What strategies are the children using to calculate the difference between two dates?

Star Maths Tools ★ Year 5

11

Clocks

Name _____ Date _____

What's the time?

- You need a partner, and you each need a copy of this sheet.
  - ☐ Use hour and minute hands to draw a time on each of the analogue clock faces and complete the am or pm options.
  - ☐ Swap your sheet with your partner.
  - ☐ Complete the correct digital times on your partner's sheet. Use 24-hour clock notation.
  - ☐ When you have both finished, take it in turns to discuss the correct answers on both sheets.

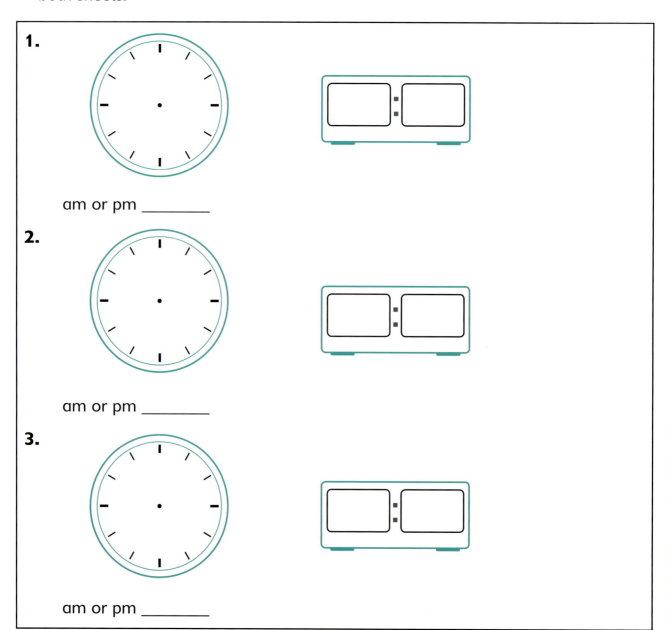

1. am or pm _____

2. am or pm _____

3. am or pm _____

12 **SCHOLASTIC**
www.scholastic.co.uk

Star Maths Tools ★ Year 5
PHOTOCOPIABLE

COORDINATES, REFLECTIONS AND ROTATIONS

This tool allows the user to plot, create and reflect shapes while also being able to show direction and coordinates by tracking a figure across the screen.

Create shapes
Click on the grid to create up to four points that automatically link to create a polygon.

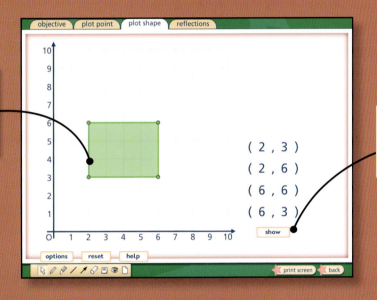

Coordinates
Click to show the coordinates of the shape.

Reflection
Select and then draw the predicted position of the reflection of the original shape.

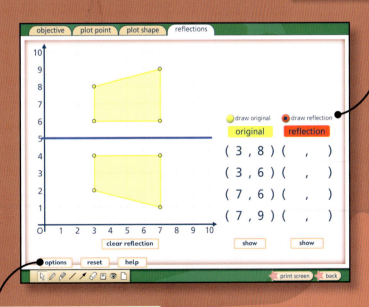

Tool functions
- Plot three- or four-sided shapes on a grid and show their coordinates
- Plot and draw reflections of shapes
- Display animation of reflection
- Select vertical, diagonal or horizontal lines of reflection

Options
Create different types of grid, draw shapes, enter coordinates or change the position of the line of reflection.

Star Maths Tools ★ Year 5

Coordinates, reflections and rotations

Activity type

Whole class

Learning objective

Understanding shape:
read and plot coordinates
in the first quadrant

Coordinates

What to do

- Open the plot point screen. In the options menu, select '1 quadrant, 0–10,' and 'person goes to random point'.
- Explain that in a pair of coordinates (x, y), the first number gives the horizontal movement or displacement, and the second the vertical movement.
- Click on the image of the person at (0, 0). Ask the children to watch carefully how the person moves along the horizontal distance and then the vertical distance.
- Ask the children to give the coordinates of the person's final position (remembering horizontal first). Check their answer by clicking 'show'. Repeat several times.
- Now go back to the options menu and choose 'enter coordinates then plot point'.
- Ask the children for a pair of points to plot. Then ask a volunteer to come to the board and mark this position. Check their answer by clicking 'plot'.
- Give the children copies of the 'coordinates' general resource sheet on the CD-ROM and ask them to plot points on the grids.

Key questions

- *What do the first and second numbers in a pair of coordinates represent?*
- *On your worksheet, can you plot the points (2, 3), (4, 5), (1, 6), (6, 1)?*

Assessment for learning

Can the children read and plot coordinates in the first quadrant?

Activity type

Whole class

Learning objective

Understanding shape:
recognise parallel and
perpendicular lines in
grids and shapes

Parallel and perpendicular lines

What to do

- Open the plot shape screen. In the options menu, select '1 quadrant, 0–10' and 'draw shape on grid'.
- Plot the points for a square or a rectangle. Start at the top left-hand vertex of the shape and move clockwise. It may help to label these points A, B, C and D (you can use the pen from the teacher's toolbox for this purpose).
- Ask the children to write the coordinates of the vertices of the shape on their individual whiteboards or sheets of paper, starting at the top left-hand corner and moving clockwise.
- Once they have done this, click 'show' to reveal the coordinates (these are given in the order they were first plotted).
- Invite the children to give you the end coordinates of two parallel lines and two perpendicular lines that make up the square.
- Repeat the activity for a different square or rectangle.

Key questions

- *What are the coordinates of the shape?*
- *Which lines are parallel and which are perpendicular?*

Assessment for learning

Do the children recognise parallel and perpendicular lines? Can they give the coordinates of the end points of the lines?

14

Star Maths Tools ★ Year 5

Coordinates, reflections and rotations

Four-sided shapes

Activity type
Group

Learning objective
Understanding shape: identify, visualise and describe properties of rectangles and regular polygons

What to do
- Open the plot shape screen. In the options menu, select '1 quadrant, 0–10' and 'draw shape on grid'.
- In groups, ask the children to draw a range of four-sided shapes (for example, a square, rectangle or quadrilateral). For each shape, ask the children about the properties of their lines and angles.
- It may help to label the vertices of the shapes A, B, C, D each time with the pen from the teacher's toolbox, so that the children can describe the lines or angles more easily.
- Give each group copies of the 'coordinates' general resource sheet on the CD-ROM to support them with this task. (You might also want to extend this activity to plotting different types of triangle.)

Key questions
- *Does this shape have any equal or parallel sides?*
- *Does this shape have any equal angles?*

Assessment for learning
Can the children identify the properties of some four-sided shapes?

Reflections

Activity type
Whole class

Learning objective
Understanding shape: draw the position of a shape after a reflection

What to do
- Open the reflections screen. In the options menu, choose '1 quadrant, 0–10', 'draw shapes on grid' and the 'horizontal' reflection line.
- Plot the points of a four-sided shape.
- Now click 'draw reflection'. Invite a volunteer to come to the board and plot the reflected shape.
- Ask the class if they think the shape plotted is correct. If not, can they suggest how it could be amended?
- Click 'reflect' to show whether their prediction is correct.
- Repeat for a range of four-sided shapes and different reflection lines.
- Provide the children with copies of photocopiable page 16. Ask them to work in pairs to create shapes for their partners to reflect.

Key questions
- *Will the reflection have the same or a different shape from the original?*
- *Look at the four vertices of the reflection you have drawn. How can you tell whether it is correct?* (Each point must be the same distance from the mirror line as the original.)

Assessment for learning
Can the children draw the position of a shape after reflection in a range of mirror lines?

Coordinates, reflections and rotations

Name _____ Date _____

Make mine the same!

- You need a partner and a copy of this sheet.
  - Draw a different four-sided shape on each grid.
  - Draw a reflection line on each grid.
  - Swap your sheet with your partner.
  - Draw in the reflections of the shapes on your partner's grid.
  - Check all of your answers together.

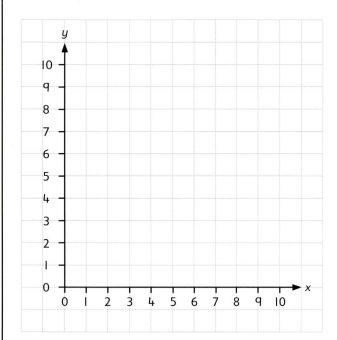 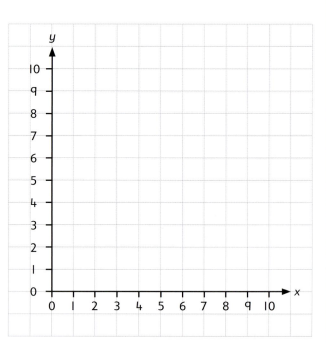

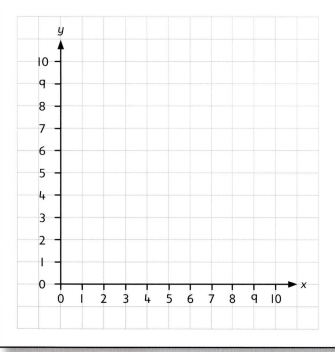 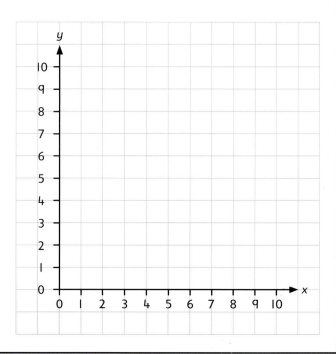

FRACTION EQUIVALENTS

This tool acts like a machine that creates equivalent fractions. The core function of the tool is to match fraction equivalents with the target fraction, helping children to visualise fractions in different formats.

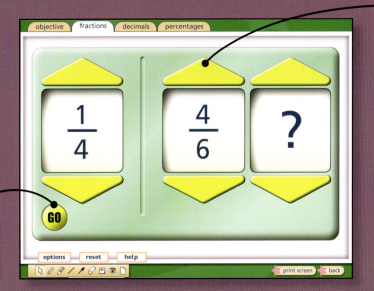

'Up' and 'down' arrows
Click to manipulate the values up or down.

Go
Click to create a random target value.

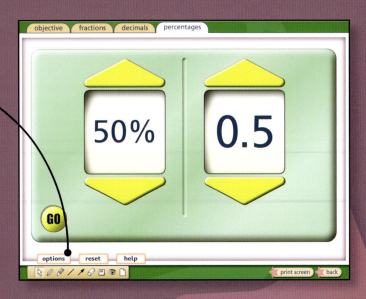

Options
Select the target and equivalent format – fraction, shape, decimal or percentage.

Tool functions

- Options to change the target and fraction equivalent
- Create a random target value
- Click the 'up' and 'down' arrows to increase or decrease the value of the equivalent fraction, shape, decimal or percentage

Star Maths Tools ★ Year 5

Fraction equivalents

Activity type

Whole class

Learning objective

Counting and understanding number: find equivalent fractions

Equivalent fractions

What to do

- In the options menu, choose 'fraction' as the target and 'fraction' and 'shape' as the equivalents.
- Explain to the children how to make an equivalent fraction. (Multiply the numerator and denominator by the same number.)
- Ask: *What do you think the equivalent fraction might be for the fraction shown?* Invite them to write their responses on individual whiteboards or sheets of paper.
- Now click the 'up' or 'down' arrows on the second barrel until the correct equivalent fraction is reached (for example $1/5 = 2/10$). Finally, click the arrows on the third barrel until the equivalent shape is displayed. This visual aid will serve to reinforce the children's basic understanding of fractions.
- Repeat the activity by clicking 'Go' to generate a new target fraction.

Key questions

- *How can you make an equivalent fraction?*
- *What fraction with a denominator of 6 is equivalent to one half?*

Assessment for learning

Do the children understand and know how to make equivalent fractions?

Activity type

Group

Learning objective

Counting and understanding number: relate fractions to their decimal representations

Relating fractions to decimals

What to do

- Give each child a copy of a 100-square (available as a general resource sheet on the CD-ROM). Explain to them that each small square represents one hundredth or 0.01.
- Ask the children to explain how they would show $27/100$ or 0.27 on the 100-square.
- In the options menu, select 'fraction' as the target and 'decimal' as the equivalent.
- Click the 'up' or 'down' arrows on the right-hand barrel until the correct decimal equivalent is found to the fraction displayed in the left-hand barrel.
- Repeat the activity by clicking 'Go' to generate a new target fraction.

Key question

- *How would you express one quarter as a decimal number?*
- *How would you show 0.56 on your 100-square?*

Assessment for learning

Can the children relate common fractions to their decimal representations?

Fraction equivalents

Activity type
Whole class

Learning objective
Counting and understanding number: relate fractions to their decimal representations; express tenths and hundredths as percentages

Percentages to decimals

What to do
- Ask: *Do you know what the word 'percentage' means?* Explain that it is a way of expressing a number as a fraction of 100.
- Tell the children that to change a percentage to a decimal means dividing the percentage by 100 – so, for example, 27% is 0.27 and 70% is 0.70 (which may be written as 0.7).
- In the options menu, choose 'percentage' as the target and 'decimal' as the equivalent.
- Click the arrows on the right-hand barrel until you reach the decimal that matches the percentage displayed in the left-hand barrel.
- Repeat the activity by clicking 'Go' to generate a new target percentage. This time, ask the children to write the decimal equivalent on their individual whiteboards (or paper) before you manipulate the right-hand barrel to reveal the answer on screen.
- Use photocopiable page 20 to provide further practice in this activity.

Key questions
- *How do you write a percentage as a decimal?*
- *How do you divide by 100?*

Assessment for learning
Can the children move comfortably between fractions, decimals and percentages?

Activity type
Review

Learning objective
Counting and understanding number: express tenths and hundredths as percentages

Percentages as fractions

What to do
- In the options menu, choose 'percentage' as the target and 'fraction' as the equivalent.
- Click the 'up' or 'down' arrows on the right-hand barrel and ask the children to say when the fraction that is shown matches the percentage displayed in the first barrel.
- Once the children have correctly matched the percentage to its equivalent fraction, click 'Go' to generate a new target percentage.

Key questions
- *What does the word 'percentage' mean?*
- *What is $1/10$ expressed as a percentage?*

Assessment for learning
Do the children understand percentages and can they express tenths and hundredths as percentages?

Fraction equivalents

Name _____ Date _____

Fill the gaps

◢ Complete the following table by filling in the equivalent percentages, fractions or decimals in each row.

Percentage	Fraction	Decimal
39%		
	$\dfrac{87}{100}$	
		0.01
50%		
	$\dfrac{9}{10}$	
		0.21
25%		
	$\dfrac{1}{5}$	
		0.3
70%		
		0.04
	$\dfrac{43}{100}$	
		0.6
75%		

20 ◨SCHOLASTIC
www.scholastic.co.uk

Star Maths Tools ★ Year 5
PHOTOCOPIABLE

GRAPHS AND CHARTS

This tool provides a range of charts and tools that are rich in data but quick to edit. A selection of prepared data sets (such as 'average temperature') allows the user to start working with the data quickly (or alternatively data can be input into blank tables). Unlike other programs, this tool allows the user to view both the chart and data table at the same time.

Scales
Scales automatically change according to the values.

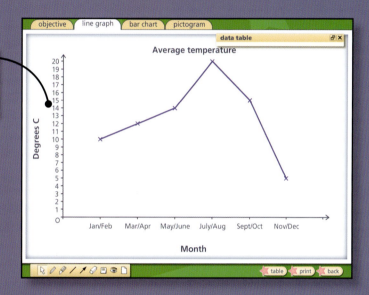

Data table
All words and numbers are editable.

Pre-set data
Select from the drop-down menu.

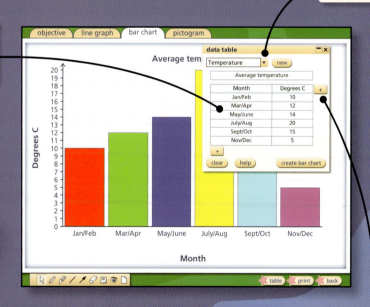

Tool functions

- Add columns or rows to the table
- Edit data
- Edit titles and labels
- Create a bar chart, line graph or pictogram
- Plot one or more charts from the data sets

'+' button
Add more rows or columns.

Graphs and charts

Understanding line graphs

Activity type: Group

Learning objective

Handling data: construct line graphs to represent changes over time; identify further questions to ask

What to do
- Open the line graph screen. Either create your own set of data or use the data already provided relating to average temperatures.
- Click 'create line graph' (in the bottom right-hand corner of the data table).
- When the on-screen graph is drawn, the data table will close. (The table can be restored by clicking on the restore icon in the top right-hand corner of the data table strip.)
- Ask the children the key questions below. (These questions refer to the line graph created about average temperature, so if you are using your own set of data they will need to be amended accordingly.)
- Repeat either by adjusting the data or by creating a new set of data.

Key questions
- *What are the maximum and minimum average temperatures shown?*
- *Do intermediate points have value on a line graph? Why?*
- *Between which months does the temperature rise the most and fall the most?*
- *Based on the data in this graph, when would you most like to go on holiday? Why?*

Assessment for learning
Can the children read a line graph and interpret information from it?

Creating bar charts

Activity type: Group

Learning objective

Handling data: answer a set of related questions by collecting, selecting and organising relevant data; draw conclusions, using ICT to present features

What to do
- Open the bar chart screen. Click 'new' in the data table.
- Collect information from the class on their favourite foods and enter this directly into the data table. The children may fill in the data themselves at the same time using photocopiable page 24.
- Question the children about an appropriate title for the data and appropriate labels for the table headings, as these will appear on the chart once it is constructed.
- Once you have entered all the data in the table, click 'create bar chart'.
- Ask the children the key questions below.
- Repeat either by adjusting the data so that the responses to questions change or by collecting further data (for example, favourite TV programmes).

Key questions
- *What is the favourite food of children in the class?*
- *How many children prefer, for example, pizza to salad?*
- *What is the least favourite food of children in the class?*

Assessment for learning
Do the children understand how to collect data? Can they present it in a chart, using ICT? Can they answer appropriate questions about the data?

Graphs and charts

Activity type
Whole class

Learning objective
Handling data: find and interpret the mode of a set of data

Finding the mode

What to do
- Open the bar chart screen. Click 'new' in the data table.
- Collect data from the children in the class on their shoe sizes and type this into the data table.
- Question the children about an appropriate title for the data and appropriate labels for the table headings as these will appear on the chart once it is constructed.
- Once you have entered all the data in the table, click 'create bar chart'.
- Explain to the children that the mode is the most popular shoe size and that it is the highest column on the bar chart. (A set of data may have more than one mode if there are two columns with the same highest value.)
- Ask the children the key questions below.
- Repeat the activity by creating a new bar chart table and collecting data relating to another topic where the mode can be readily identified.

Key questions
- *What shoe size is represented by the highest column in the bar chart?*
- *Which shoe size represents the mode of the set of data?*
- *Who might this information be useful to?* (Shoe manufacturers and shoe shops.)

Assessment for learning
Can children find the mode of a set of data using a bar chart and interpret its meaning?

Activity type
Group

Learning objective
Handling data: draw conclusions, using ICT to present features, and identify further questions to ask

Interpreting pictograms

What to do
- Open the pictogram screen.
- Tell the children that a number of people were asked in a survey about how they got to work and this is represented in a pictogram.
- Insert into the pictogram a different number of red squares in each row.
- Label the chart 'Transport survey'. Type the different types of transport in the vertical labels on the left-hand side of the pictogram (walk, car, bicycle, bus, taxi, motorcycle) and label the x-axis 'Number of people'. Explain that each shape represents five people. Type this into the key.
- Ask the children the key questions below.
- Repeat by either constructing a new pictogram or by saying that each shape now represents, for example, two people.

Key questions
- *How many people use a motorcycle as their main means of transport?*
- *What is the total number of people who took part in the survey?*

Assessment for learning
Can the children interpret a pictogram when a symbol represents numbers or quantities other than 1?

Graphs and charts

Name _____ Date _____

Data table

Title: _____

Date of data collection: _____

Horizontal axis labels	Tally	Tally total	Vertical axis label

24 **SCHOLASTIC**
www.scholastic.co.uk

Star Maths Tools ★ Year 5
PHOTOCOPIABLE

MAGIC CALCULATOR

The magic calculator is a large-scale standard calculator with a range of additional functions. Calculations, as input by the user, can be read as on a standard calculator or shown as a vertical or horizontal equation. The magic calculator has an additional button, the 'magic button', which creates pre-defined numbers on the screen to support the user in creating examples.

Calculator
A complete set of standard buttons available on most calculators.

Results
These can be shown vertically or horizontally.

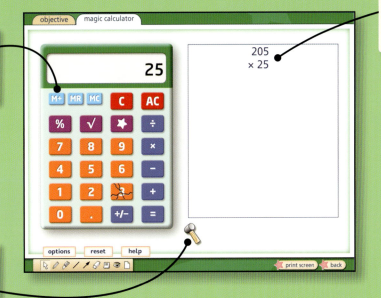

Hammer
Drag the hammer to selected keys on the calculator to disable them.

Magic number
Pre-define to include negative numbers and decimals as required.

Options
Show number sentences vertically or horizontally next to the calculator.

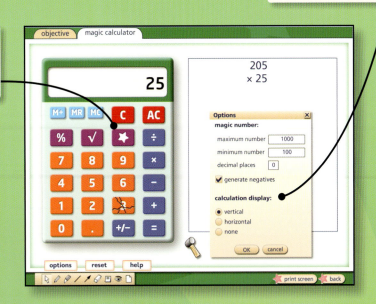

Tool functions

- 0–9 number buttons
- Memory buttons
- Percentage and specific function buttons
- The six basic function buttons
- Hammer to disable keys
- Magic button creates a random number within specified parameters

Star Maths Tools ★ Year 5

Magic calculator

Activity type

Whole class

Learning objective

Calculating: use a calculator to solve problems, including those involving fractions; interpret the display correctly in the context of measurement

Finding fractions

What to do

- Remind the children that three quarters is 3 ÷ 4 and that 'of' means *multiply*.
- Explain that to find three quarters of £150 on the calculator requires the calculation 3 ÷ 4 × 150. Alternatively, find ¼ first and then multiply by 3 to find ¾. Use the on-screen calculator to demonstrate the steps of the calculation.
- The result of the calculation may need interpretation. Ask the children how they would interpret this answer. In this case the calculator gives 112.5, so the answer to three quarters of £150 is £112.50.
- Repeat, using examples in the context of money or measurement. Ensure that the children are aware of the need to interpret the calculator answer.

Key questions

- *When using a calculator, how would you input 'three quarters'?*
- *In the context of money, how do you write 112.5 so that it reads as an amount of money?*

Assessment for learning

Can the children find a fraction of a quantity, using a calculator, and interpret the display in context?

Activity type

Group

Learning objective

Calculating: use understanding of place value to multiply whole numbers by 10, 100 or 1000

Multiplying by 10, 100 or 1000

What to do

- Remind the children that multiplying by 10 makes a number 10 times larger, by 100 makes numbers 100 times larger, and by 1000 makes numbers 1000 times larger.
- Key '3' into the calculator and multiply this by 10, 100, and 1000. Click 'clear' between each calculation. Each time, ask the children to write their answers on their individual whiteboards (or sheets of paper) before pressing '='. If you wish, use the pen from the teacher's toolbox to draw a place value grid to show how the digits move when multiplying by 10, 100 and 1000.
- Repeat this process, using numbers such as 45, so that when multiplying by 10, 5 becomes 50 and 40 becomes 400 – resulting in 450. If necessary, use the on-screen notepad to show how the number 45 can be partitioned into ones and tens.
- Repeat by multiplying a range of numbers from ones to hundreds. Depending on the children's ability, you might also want to include decimal numbers.
- Give the children copies of photocopiable page 28, which provides extra support for this activity.

Key questions

- *If a number is multiplied by 100, how much larger does it become?*
- *If 40 is multiplied by 1000, what is the answer?*

Assessment for learning

Do the children understand how to multiply whole numbers by 10, 100, or 1000?

26

Star Maths Tools ★ Year 5

Magic calculator

Activity type
Group

Learning objective
Calculating: use understanding of place value to divide whole numbers by 10 or 100

Dividing by 10 or 100

What to do
- Remind the children that dividing by 10 makes a number 10 times smaller and dividing by 100 makes numbers 100 times smaller. Consequently, dividing 3 by 10 results in 0.3 or $^3/_{10}$ and dividing 3 by 100 results in 0.03 or $^3/_{100}$.
- Demonstrate these calculations on the calculator. If you wish, use the pen from the teacher's toolbox to draw a place value grid to show how the digits move when dividing by 10 and 100.
- Now divide 70 by 10 and 100 and demonstrate that 70 ÷ 10 = 7, which is one-tenth, and 70 ÷ 100 = 0.7, which is one-hundredth.
- Next, divide 73 by 10 and 100 and discuss the answers.
- Repeat, using a range of numbers. To generate new numbers quickly and easily, use the 'magic button' on the calculator (appropriate parameters can be set in the options menu).
- Hand out copies of photocopiable page 28 to provide extra support for this activity.

Key questions
- *When dividing by 10, does the answer become larger or smaller?*
- *If dividing 85 by 10 or 100, what is the result?*

Assessment for learning
Do the children understand place value and what happens when whole numbers are divided by 10 or 100?

Activity type
Whole class

Learning objective
Calculating: find percentages of numbers

Finding percentages

What to do
- Pose the question: *What is 10% of 80?* Ask the children what they think the answer might be.
- Explain that 10% is equivalent to $^1/_{10}$ and $^1/_{10}$ of 80 is $^8/_{10}$ = 8.
- Explain how to use the percentage key on the calculator to check the children's answers. Demonstrate this, by keying in 80 × 10% = 8.
- Next, demonstrate some other examples, such as 10% of 70 or 10% of 600.
- Explain that 20%, 30%... are twice, three times... as much as 10%.
- Ask the children to find 10% of 60. Use the hammer to disable the 2 and 3 buttons on the calculator. Now ask the children to find 20% of 60 and 30% of 60 without a calculator. Once they have done this, reset the calculator (with the 2 and 3 buttons mended), to check their results.

Key questions
- *How do you find 10% of a number?*
- *If you know 10%, how do you find 20%, 30%...?*

Assessment for learning
Can the children find 10%, 20%, 30%... of a number and use a calculator to check their results?

Magic calculator

Missing numbers

Name _____ Date _____

- Fill in the missing numbers in the table.
- Use a calculator to check your answers.

Number	× 10	× 100	× 1000	÷ 10	÷ 100
5					
7			7000		
9					
10					
20	200				
50					
72				7.2	
84					0.84
96					
47					
100					
156				15.6	
179					
225		22,500			
268					
586					

28 **SCHOLASTIC**
www.scholastic.co.uk

Star Maths Tools ★ Year 5
PHOTOCOPIABLE

NUMBER LINE

This tool enables the user to incorporate all common units of measurement (including time, money, weights and lengths) within a defined number range. The green scroll buttons allow scrolling forward and backwards indefinitely or, by selecting the options button, to defined maximum or minimum numbers. The value markers can be used to identify parts of a sequence or to create number ranges.

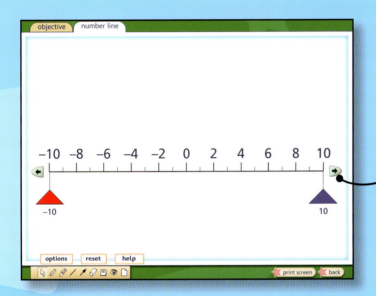

Scroll
- Scroll forward or backwards either indefinitely or between pre-set limits.
- The numbers will go below 0 to show negative numbers.

Measurements
Create number lines that reflect length, weight, time or money.

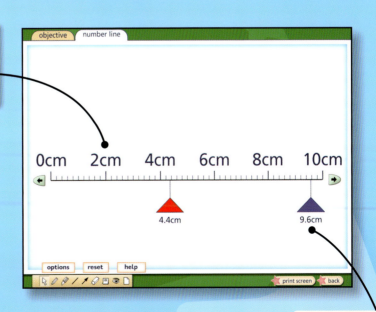

Marker values
Show or hide marker values.

Tool functions

- Forward and reverse scrolling of numbers
- Range of sub-divisions available
- Ability to add £, hour, mins, secs, m, cm, l, ml, g, kg into the units box
- Hide or show marker values
- Hide or show digits on number line

Number line

Activity type

Starter

Learning objective

Counting and understanding number: count from any given number in whole-number and decimal steps, extending beyond zero when counting backwards

Counting beyond zero

What to do
- In the options menu, select start number '-10', end number '10', step '1', sub-divisions '2', 'show numbers' and 'show marker values'.
- Move the red and blue value markers to -8.5 and 8.5 respectively.
- Starting at 8.5, count backwards with the whole class from 8.5 to 7.5, down to -8.5.
- Repeat, starting at a different decimal number.
- Move the right-hand marker to 1.5 and ask the first question below. Continue with similar questions.
- If the children are ready, change the step size to 10 in the options menu and introduce other decimal numbers.

Key questions
- *What is 4 less than 1.5?*
- *What is 6 more than -3.5?* (Move the left-hand marker to -3.5 to start counting.)

Assessment for learning
Can the children count beyond zero in decimal steps using the number line?

Activity type

Whole class

Learning objective

Knowing and using number facts: use knowledge of place value and addition and subtraction of two-digit numbers to derive sums and differences of decimals

Decimal pairs that add to 10

What to do
- In the options menu, select start number '0', end number '10', step '1', sub-divisions '10', 'show numbers'.
- Check that the children understand that each sub-division is worth 0.1.
- With the marker values hidden, move each marker several times and check that the children can read and understand the value of any number on the line.
- Reveal the marker values and move the left-hand marker along the line to, for example, 3.6.
- Explain to the children that by adding on along the line they are going to find the number that, when added to 3.6, will give 10.
- Show the children how to add on to the next whole number and then find the whole number needed to give 10.
- After several examples, give the children their own number line questions on photocopiable page 32 to complete in pairs. Extend the number range beyond 10 in subsequent sessions.

Key questions
- *What is the decimal number needed to reach the next whole number?*
- *What is the number needed to reach 10?*
- *Can you write down the number pair that adds to 10?*

Assessment for learning
Can the children quickly derive pairs of numbers with one decimal place that total 10?

Number line

Activity type
Whole class

Learning objective
Counting and understanding number: explain what each digit represents in a number with up to two decimal places, and round these numbers

Rounding to the nearest number

What to do
- In the options menu, select start number '0', end number '20', step '1', sub-divisions '10', 'show numbers'.
- With the marker values hidden, move the left-hand marker along the line so that it is between two whole numbers, but closer to one number than the other.
- Ask the children to say which is the nearest whole number. Remind them that 'rounding' means making an estimate of that number to the nearest whole number.
- Now show the marker number and repeat the process.
- Remind the children that if the tenths digit is 4 or less, then the number is rounded down. If the tenths digit is 5 or more, then the number is rounded up. Demonstrate at the same time the closeness of each number to the nearest whole number on the line.
- Give the children some calculations (such as 3.6 × 4.3) to do on a calculator. Ask them first to estimate their answers by rounding each number.

Key questions
- *When you're rounding 3.5 to the nearest number, would you round up or down?*
- *Estimate the answer to 5.4 × 4.9.*

Assessment for learning
Do the children understand rounding to the nearest whole number? Can they use this to check their calculations?

Activity type
Starter

Learning objective
Measuring: interpret a reading that lies between two unnumbered divisions on a scale

Reading partially labelled scales

What to do
- In the options menu, select start number '0', end number '10', step '1', sub-divisions 'none, 'show numbers' and units 'cm'.
- Explain that this ruler only measures in centimetres but that the children have to estimate measurements as accurately as possible in millimetres.
- Move either marker and ask the children to estimate the measurement to the nearest millimetre.
- Once they have agreed on their estimation, go back to the options menu, select sub-divisions '10' and 'show marker values', to check how close the children's estimation was to the actual measurement.
- Repeat with a new 'ruler' by changing the end number to 20.

Key questions
- *Is the marker more or less than halfway between the whole numbers of centimetres?*
- *What is your estimate of the measurement?*

Assessment for learning
Can the children interpret the reading on a ruler between unnumbered divisions?

Star Maths Tools ★ Year 5

Number line

Name _____   Date _____

Totals to 10

- You need a partner, and you each need a copy of this sheet.
- In the 'First number' column, write four numbers that each have one decimal place. Each number must be less than 10.
- Swap your sheet with your partner.
- Complete the 'Second number' column and the calculations in the last column. Use the blank number lines provided below to check your answers.
- When you have both finished, check each other's answers.

	First number	Second number	
Example	3.6	6.4	3.6 + 6.4 = 10
1			+ = 10
2			+ = 10
3			+ = 10
4			+ = 10

1.

2.

3.

4.

NUMBER SQUARE

This tool is a flexible version of the familiar number square, and includes 100-square, addition square and multiplication square options. The user is able to adjust the shape of the square and the number range to create the specific resource they require. The grids can also be printed out for individual or class use.

Options
Create bespoke squares quickly using the pre-set numbers.

Grid tools
Change background colour, hide, highlight, edit and drag squares off the grid.

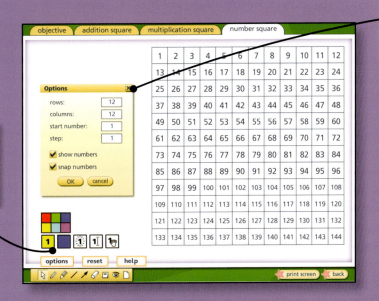

Numbers
- Drag numbers from the grid.
- Input numbers into the grid.

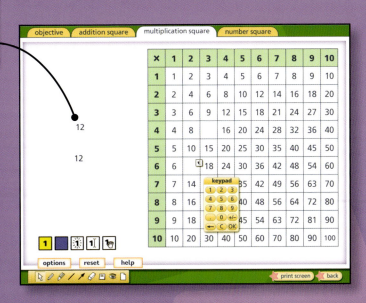

Tool functions

- Columns and rows adjustable
- Start number adjustable
- Highlight, hide and reveal buttons
- Step number adjustable
- Hide/reveal individual numbers or whole rows
- Print grid
- Drag numbers off the square
- Input numbers into the square

Star Maths Tools ★ Year 5

33

Number square

Pairs of factors

Activity type

Whole class

Learning objective

Knowing and using number facts: identify pairs of factors of two-digit whole numbers

What to do

- Open the multiplication square. In the options menu, select rows '12', columns '12', start number '1' and step '1'.
- Ask the children to identify each place in the multiplication square where the number 24 occurs. Drag each of these numbers and drop them in the area outside the grid.
- Explain what is meant by 'a factor of 24': a number that divides into 24 without a remainder.
- By looking at the blank squares in the table, ask the children to tell you all the numbers that are factors of 24, and the pairs of factors.
- Repeat the activity, using other numbers – for example, 18, 20, 30, 36 and so on.

Key questions

- *What are the factors of 24?*
- *What does the word 'factor' mean?*

Assessment for learning

Do the children understand what is meant by a factor? Can they find factors of numbers up to 100?

Times tables

Activity type

Starter

Learning objective

Knowing and using number facts: recall quickly multiplication facts up to 10 × 10

What to do

- Open the multiplication square. In the options menu, select rows '10', columns '10', start number '1' and step '1'.
- Use the blue 'hide' button to hide the first row and column of the square (the green headings).
- Highlight a number (for example, 40) and ask the children to tell you which numbers multiplied together give 40.
- Repeat the activity, using different numbers.

Key questions

- *Are there any other numbers that can be multiplied together to give 40?*
- *Are there numbers not shown on the table square which can be multiplied together to give 40?*

Assessment for learning

Can the children quickly recall their multiplication facts? Do they understand that there is often more than one way of giving the product of a number?

34

Star Maths Tools ★ Year 5

Number square

Activity type
Paired assessment

Learning objective
Using and applying mathematics: explore patterns, properties and relationships and propose a general statement involving numbers

Number investigation

What to do
- Open the addition square. In the options menu, select rows '10', columns '10', start number '1' and step '1'.
- Highlight a number (for example, 11). Ask the children what happens when they add the two numbers above and below 11, the two numbers next to 11 on each diagonal, and the numbers horizontally on either side of 11.
- Ask the children about their results.
- Highlight a different number and ask the children to work out the answers for this and several other highlighted numbers (or numbers of their own choice).
- Provide the children with copies of photocopiable page 36 to support them with this activity.

Key questions
- *What happens each time you add the two numbers horizontally and vertically and diagonally next to a highlighted number in the addition square?*
- *Can you give a rule to say what happens?*

Assessment for learning
Can the children recognise number relationships and make a statement giving a general rule? (NB At this level it is sufficient to say that the numbers added are always twice the highlighted number.)

Activity type
Starter

Learning objective
Using and applying mathematics: explore patterns, properties and relationships and propose a general statement involving numbers

Mystery squares

What to do
- Open the number square. In the options menu, select rows '10', columns '10', start number '2' and step '2'. This means that each number is increasing by 2 each time.
- Hide the whole square. Explain that the children have to discover all the numbers.
- Reveal one number and ask the children what the numbers next to this might be.
- Reveal the adjacent numbers to see if the children were correct. Then ask them what other numbers they would next like to reveal in the square. Show them the results.
- Ask the children if they can say what is happening in the number square. When they are correct, reveal the whole square by clicking 'reset'.
- Repeat the activity, using number squares with different start and step numbers, or the addition and multiplication squares.

Key questions
- *What number is it helpful to reveal early on?* (The first number in the square.)
- *Which row is it helpful to reveal first?*

Assessment for learning
Can the children make predictions and test and check their results?

Star Maths Tools ★ Year 5   35

Number square

Name _____ Date _____

Addition square

+	1	2	3	4	5	6	7	8	9	10
1	2	3	4	5	6	7	8	9	10	11
2	3	4	5	6	7	8	9	10	11	12
3	4	5	6	7	8	9	10	11	12	13
4	5	6	7	8	9	10	11	12	13	14
5	6	7	8	9	10	11	12	13	14	15
6	7	8	9	10	11	12	13	14	15	16
7	8	9	10	11	12	13	14	15	16	17
8	9	10	11	12	13	14	15	16	17	18
9	10	11	12	13	14	15	16	17	18	19
10	11	12	13	14	15	16	17	18	19	20

36 **SCHOLASTIC**
www.scholastic.co.uk

Star Maths Tools ★ Year 5
PHOTOCOPIABLE

NUMBER WORDS

This tool allows the user to create numbers in words from numbers with up to three decimal points to hundreds of thousands. Included in the program is a randomiser that will create a range of random numbers within any given parameters.

Set number
Input numbers manually or use the 'random' function.

Tabs
Select parameters for numbers.

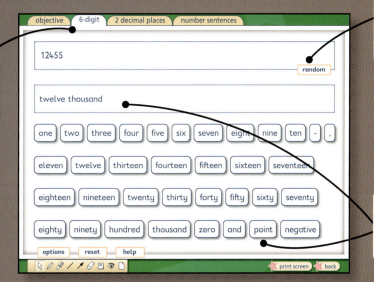

Number cards
Drag into the lower box to make a sentence.

Options
The options button allows the question to be reversed.

Tool functions

- Drag and drop number names
- Drag and drop numbers
- Input box for defined numbers
- 'Random' button generates a range of numbers

Star Maths Tools ✶ Year 5

Number words

Activity type

Whole class

Learning objective

Counting and understanding number: explain what each digit represents in whole numbers

Whole numbers up to 100,000

What to do

- Click on the '6-digit' tab at the top of the screen. In the options menu, select 'use word cards'.
- Click in the top box on the screen and type in a number (or click the 'random' button to generate a random six-digit number).
- Ask the children the key questions below and then invite them to write the number in words on their individual whiteboards or sheets of paper.
- Once they have done this, drag and drop the appropriate number words into the second box on the screen to make the number.
- Now reverse the process by using the number word cards to write a number in the bottom box, and asking the children to write the same number in numerals.
- Hand out copies of photocopiable page 40. Ask the children to work in pairs to complete the grids.

Key questions

- *What is the place value of the second digit in the number?*
- *What is the place value of the fourth digit in the number?*

Assessment for learning

Can the children use numerals and words to explain what the digits in whole numbers represent?

Activity type

Whole class

Learning objective

Counting and understanding number: explain what each digit represents in decimals with up to two places

Reading decimals

What to do

- Click on the '2 decimal places' tab. In the options menu, select 'use word cards'.
- Click in the top box and type in a number with one or two decimal places (or click the 'random' button to generate a number with two decimal places).
- Ask the children the key questions below, then ask them to write the number in words on their individual whiteboards or sheets of paper.
- Once they have done this, drag and drop the relevent words onto the screen to make the number.
- Now reverse the process by using the number word cards to write a number in the bottom box, and asking the children to write the number in numerals.

Key questions

- *What is the place value of the first digit to the left of the decimal point? How would you say this part of the number?*
- *What is the place value of the second digit to the left of the decimal point? How would you say this part of the number?*

Assessment for learning

Can the children use numerals and words to explain what the digits in numbers with two decimal places represent?

38

Star Maths Tools ★ Year 5

Number words

Activity type
Starter

Learning objective
Using and applying mathematics: explore patterns, properties and relationships involving numbers

Find the missing numbers

What to do
- Click on the 'number sentences' tab at the top of the screen.
- Drag the relevant cards provided at the foot of the screen to form the number sentence 2☐ + △ = 14 in the top box.
- Ask the children to write down on their individual whiteboards (or sheets of paper) what numbers the square and the triangle might represent. Once they have done this, ask them to hold up their whiteboards to show you.
- Discuss the children's responses. Ask the key questions below.
- Drag the relevant cards to show some solutions in the blank boxes on the screen.
- Explore other number patterns, using the cards to create a range of different number sentences for the children to solve.

Key questions
- *Is there more than one solution to the problem?*
- *What do you notice about the numbers represented by the square and triangle?* (As one number increases the other decreases.)

Assessment for learning
Can the children solve a problem by finding patterns in numbers?

Activity type
Starter

Learning objective
Using and applying mathematics: explore patterns, properties and relationships and propose a general statement involving numbers

Exploring number patterns

What to do
- Click on the 'number sentences' tab.
- Drag the relevant cards into the top box to form the following sequence, using the blank card to separate each number: 1 3 5 7 9
- Ask the children the key questions below.
- Repeat the activity using other sequences such as:
  2 4 6 8
  1 2 4 8
  20 17 14 11
  80 40 20…

Key questions
- *What are the next two numbers in the sequence?*
- *Can you describe what is happening to the numbers in the sequence?*

Assessment for learning
Can the children explore patterns and find a general relationship involving numbers?

Star Maths Tools ★ Year 5

39

Number words

Name _____ Date _____

Name that number

■ You need a partner, and you each need a copy of this sheet.

❑ Write numbers in the first column of each table. Remember to include some numbers with decimals as well as whole numbers.

❑ Swap your sheet with your partner.

❑ Write the answers in the second column.

❑ When you have both finished, check your answers together.

Numbers (digits)	Numbers in words
Example: 32,457	thirty two thousand, four hundred and fifty seven

Numbers in words	Numbers (digits)
Example: forty three point one seven	43.17

40 ■SCHOLASTIC
www.scholastic.co.uk

Star Maths Tools ★ Year 5
PHOTOCOPIABLE

PARTITION NUMBERS

This tool allows the user to show a number as place value arrow cards, which can be separated to partition the number. Each 'arrow card' is a different colour to help users identify each part. The name of each part can also be shown in words.

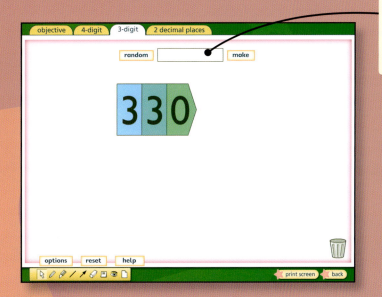

Create partition number
- Input number manually or use the 'random' function.
- Click on 'make' to create the partition cards.

Drop-down menu
Click on the arrow to reveal the number's name.

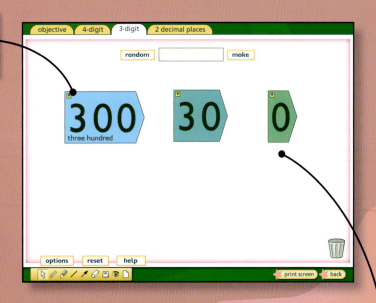

Tool functions

- Create any number and then 'make'
- Randomly create a number within pre-defined parameters
- Partition all parts of the number
- Reveal the number's name
- Pull the numbers apart, then snap them back to each other

Partition cards
All numbers can be pulled apart and then repositioned.

Star Maths Tools ★ Year 5

Partition numbers

Activity type

Whole class

Learning objective

Counting and understanding number: explain what each digit represents in whole numbers and decimals with up to two places

Explaining two decimal places

What to do

- Open the '4-digit' screen. In the options menu, select decimal places '2'.
- Type in a number (for example, 3.42) and click 'make'.
- Ask the children what each digit represents in turn - for example, '3 units'. Ask the children to write this on their individual whiteboards or sheets of paper.
- To check their results, drag and drop the different parts of the number so that it is shown as units, tenths and hundredths. Explain the values of the position of digits to the right of the decimal point.
- Now put the parts back together, and ask the children again what each digit represents.
- Repeat by typing in a range of other numbers (or click the 'random' button to automatically generate numbers with two decimal places).
- Ask the children to work in pairs to complete the grid on photocopiable page 44.

Key questions

- *What does each digit in the number represent?*
- *Can you write $^3/_{10}$ and $^7/_{100}$ as decimals?*

Assessment for learning

Can the children explain what each digit represents in a number with two decimal places?

Activity type

Group

Learning objective

Calculating: refine and use efficient written methods to multiply HTU × U

Multiplication

What to do

- Open the '3-digit' screen. In the options menu, select decimal places 'none'.
- Type in a number (for example, 124) and click 'make'. Then type in 4 and click 'make'.
- Ask the children to partition 124 into hundreds, tens and units on their individual whiteboards or sheets of paper.
- Check their answers by dragging the first number apart to partition it and position the second number (4) in the middle beneath the partitioned number.
- Explain to the children that the 4 must be used to multiply all parts of the partition.
- Using the pen from the teacher's toolbox to show your calculations on screen, multiply each part of the partitioned number: 4 × 4, 4 × 20, 4 × 100. Write the results beneath one another in place value columns.
- Ask the children to add the result on their individual whiteboards and write their result as 124 × 4 = 496.

Key questions

- *What does each digit in 124 represent?*
- *How do you think you could multiply the number 124 by 4?*

Assessment for learning

Can the children use partitioning to multiply a three-digit number by a one-digit number?

42

Star Maths Tools ★ Year 5

Partition numbers

Activity type

Whole class

Learning objective

Calculating: use efficient written methods to add whole numbers and decimals with up to two places

Adding decimal numbers

What to do
- Open the '2 decimal places' screen.
- Type in 2.64 and click 'make'. Repeat for 4.5. Drag and partition each number, setting digits with the same place value beneath each other.
- Explain that tenths must be added to tenths and units to units.
- Ask the children to do the addition on their individual whiteboards.
- Explain that adding 0.6 and 0.5 gives the answer 1.1 so there is another 1 to be added to the units digit.
- Explain that when adding decimal numbers, the decimal points in each number must always be placed beneath one another so that digits remain in the correct place value columns.
- Use the pen from the teacher's toolbox to write the sum of the two numbers as a column addition. Ask the children to write this on their individual whiteboards.

Key questions
- *What is the place value of each digit in the first number?*
- *Why is it important to keep the decimal points underneath one another when adding two decimals?*

Assessment for learning
Can the children use efficient written methods to add whole numbers and decimals with up to two decimal places?

Activity type

Starter

Learning objective

Counting and understanding number: explain what each digit represents in whole numbers and decimals with up to two places, and order these numbers

Larger or smaller

What to do
- Open the '2 decimal places' screen. Click 'random' and 'make' twice to create two numbers on arrow cards.
- Explain that the larger number is the number with the greatest number of tens.
- Now type in two numbers that have the same number of tens and units - for example, 16.5 and 16.49.
- Partition both numbers and explain that if the tens and units are the same then the largest number is the number with the greatest number of tenths.
- Type in more numbers that are similar and check by partitioning. (The most difficult pairs for children are those in which one number shows only tenths.)

Key questions
- *When you compare three-digit numbers (numbers with hundreds, tens and units), how do you know which is the larger?*
- *Which is larger: one tenth or one hundredth?*

Assessment for learning
Can the children order two numbers with decimals up to two places?

Star Maths Tools ★ Year 5

43

Partition numbers

Name _____ Date _____

Digits and decimals

■ You need a partner and one copy of this sheet between you.

☐ Take it in turn to choose one of these numbers.

☐ Tell your partner what each digit represents. Then write each digit in the correct place in the table below. The first one has been done for you as an example.

☐ When you have finished, make up more numbers for each other.

Number	Thousands	Hundreds	Tens	Units	.	Tenths	Hundredths
24.3			2	4		3	
157.9							
2984.19							
12.63							
0.05							
0.7							
1.37							
1444.73							
3000.54							
3786.00							
231.7							
638.04							
2.8							
1.03							
700.4							

44 ■SCHOLASTIC
www.scholastic.co.uk

Star Maths Tools ★ Year 5
PHOTOCOPIABLE

SHAPE PAPER

This tool allows the user to draw complex polygons on the screen. By clicking on the yellow corner points, the shapes can be stretched to form a range of quadrilaterals, triangles and lines. Polygons can also be combined to create more complex shapes or nets. Accurate measurements can be taken using the protractor and ruler.

More than four sides
To create a shape with more than four sides, grab the middle of any line and drag, automatically creating a new point. To remove any point, drag it to a neighbouring point and drop it onto it.

Create a polygon
The grid creates up to four points that automatically link to create a polygon as the user selects parts of the screen.

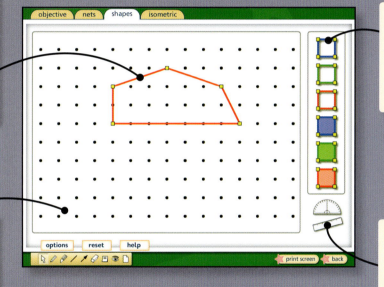

Grid types
The tool opens with 1 cm square paper but other types of paper can be selected.

Measurement
A ruler and protractor can be dragged onto the screen.

Joining shapes
Shapes can be dragged from the shape palette and will snap next to existing shapes for accurate images.

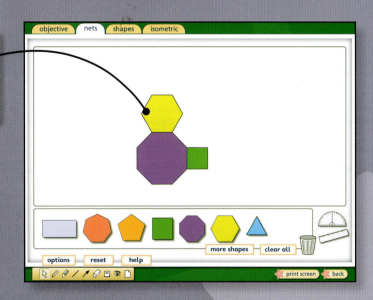

Tool functions

- Polygons
- Solid polygons
- Shapes
- Ruler
- Protractor
- Various types of background paper

Star Maths Tools ★ Year 5

Shape paper

Activity type

Whole class

Learning objective

Understanding shape: identify and draw nets of 3D shapes

Nets of a cube

What to do

- Open the nets screen. Explain that the aim of the activity is find out whether shapes made up of squares can be folded to form a cube.
- Drag six squares from the palette at the foot of the screen and fix them together. (Some suggestions for different formations are given on photocopiable page 48.)
- Using a cube, demonstrate to the children what is meant by a 'net'.
- Ask: *Would you be able to fold the shape into a cube?* If the children are able to do this, then the shape is a net of a cube. Invite a volunteer to come to the whiteboard and explain why the shape may form a net or not.
- Repeat the activity, using other shapes made from six squares. Print out the sets of shapes that are made and invite the children to try cutting and folding them to check whether their predictions are correct.
- Hand out copies of photocopiable page 48 to provide the children with further practice in folding nets to form cubes.

Key questions

- *How many faces has a cube?*
- *Can this shape be folded to form a cube?*

Assessment for learning

Can the children identify the net of a cube both practically and visually?

Activity type

Group

Learning objective

Using and applying mathematics: explore patterns, properties and relationships involving shapes

Tessellating patterns

What to do

- Open the nets screen. Make sure that the default setting of 'snap shapes to each other' and 'allow rotation' is activated in the options menu.
- Ask: *Do you know what a tessellating pattern is?*
- Invite volunteers to come to the board to try making patterns using several single shapes (for example, ten equilateral triangles), by dragging the shapes from the palette, dropping them onto the working space and then snapping them together to form a pattern. Ask: *Which shapes tessellate on their own*?
- Next, experiment with combinations of different shapes.
- Ask the children to record on their individual whiteboards or sheets of paper which shapes will tessellate.

Key questions

- *What does it mean if a shape tessellates?*
- *Which shapes tessellate on their own and which need a second shape to form a tessellating pattern?*

Assessment for learning

Can the children use trial and error to explore properties, patterns and relationships between shapes?

46

Star Maths Tools ★ Year 5

Shape paper

Activity type
Starter

Learning objective
Understanding shape: complete patterns with up to two lines of symmetry

Lines of symmetry

What to do
- Open the nets screen.
- Drag any of the shapes from the palette at the foot of the screen onto the working space. Ask: *How many lines of symmetry does this shape have?* Use the pen from the teacher's toolbox to draw these lines on the shape.
- Next, invite a child to come to the board and add another shape to the first one (the second shape may be the same or different).
- Ask the class how many lines of symmetry the new shape has. After discussing the children's suggestions, draw these lines (if any) on the shape.
- Repeat the activity, using a range of different shapes from the palette.

Key questions
- *How many lines of symmetry does the new shape have?*
- *If you added another shape that was the same, would the number of lines of symmetry change?* (This would depend on where it was placed as well as the shape added.)

Assessment for learning
Can the children complete patterns and make shapes with up to two lines of symmetry?

Activity type
Whole class

Learning objective
Measuring: use the formula for the area of a rectangle to calculate the rectangle's area

Finding the area of rectangles

What to do
- Open the shapes screen.
- Create several different-shaped rectangles by dragging and dropping the shapes provided on the right-hand side of the screen onto the grid. The shape of each quadrilateral can be altered by clicking on the corner points and dragging them to the desired position on the grid.
- Calculate the area of each shape by counting the number of squares it covers on the grid.
- Using a sticky note from the teacher's toolbox, make a note of the length, width and area of each rectangle.
- Ask the children if they can find a relationship between the length, width and area. If they can't, try some more rectangles.
- Once the relationship (area = length × width) is established, check the result by counting squares and then applying the equation.

Key questions
- *Can you find the area of this rectangle by counting squares?*
- *Can you describe the relationship between length, width and area?*

Assessment for learning
Do the children understand how the formula for the area of a rectangle is derived? Can they use this to calculate the area?

Find the cubes

◼ You need a pair of scissors.

☐ Cut out each shape.

☐ Fold along the dotted lines.

☐ Which of the shapes are nets of a cube?

1.

2.

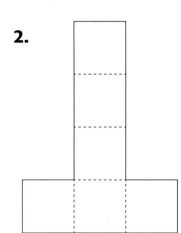

3.

4.

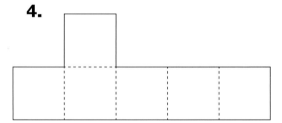

5.